# THE AWESOME ORIGAMI PACK

**BARRON'S**

First edition for the United States and Canada
published in 2014 by Barron's Educational Series, Inc.

Copyright © 2014 Linda Cole Books Ltd.

Created by Linda Cole Books Ltd., London, U.K.
Design: Miranda Brown, The Book Makers Ltd., U.K.
Editor: Elise See Tai

Written by Nick Robinson
All diagrams copyright Nick Robinson
Models of the fish and the four-pointed star copyright Nick Robinson
All other models based on traditional designs.

All inquiries should be addressed to:
Barron's Educational Series, Inc.
250 Wireless Boulevard, Hauppauge, New York 11788
**www.barronseduc.com**

ISBN: 978-0-7641-6726-3
Library of Congress Control Number: 2014930457

Manufactured in China by Main Choice Printing, Dong Guan
Date of Manufacture: June 2014
9 8 7 6 5 4 3 2 1

Product conforms to all CPSC and CPSIA 2008 standards.
No lead or phthalate hazard.

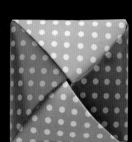

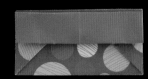

# Contents

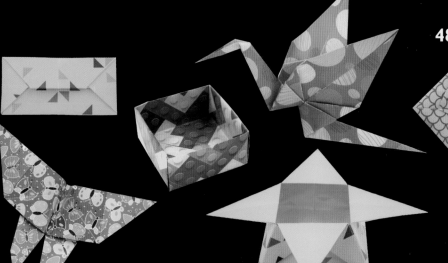

# Folding guide

Folding paper neatly doesn't always come easily to people new to origami. However, it is possible for everyone to create impressive models, as long as you follow these few simple folding tips.

## Folding tips

### Take it slowly
Fold slowly—it's not a race. The results will outweigh any extra time taken during the folding sequence.

### Setting up
Fold at a well-lit table, with space to fold and to follow the instructions in the book.

### Position carefully
Make all creases nice and sharp, but make sure the paper is perfectly positioned before flattening it.

### Practice
Practice and make each model three times with scrap paper before using the beautiful paper supplied with the pack.

### Share it!
Folding in a small group makes origami even more fun. Teach a model to your friends—it will really help your understanding of the folding sequence.

## Using the folding guide
If you have not tried folding paper before, start to practice folding by using the guide on the inside back cover of this book. It will help you fold the papers in your pack accurately. The yellow lines show you the half and quarter folds, the blue lines show you the thirds, and the orange lines show the diagonal folds.

FOLDING GUIDE

THIRD

THIRD

QUARTER

HALF

QUARTER

HALF

## Key to symbols:

### Folds

- - - - - - - - -

**Valley fold**
**(see right)**

—·—·—·—·—·—·

**Mountain fold**
**(see right)**

─────────────

**Previous fold**

### Instructions

 **Turn the paper over**

 **Repeat underneath**

 **Repeat steps**

**x3**

 **Press or push in**

 **Rotate the paper**

 **Take care**

### Difficulty

**Simple Trickier Complex Challenging**

# Basic folds

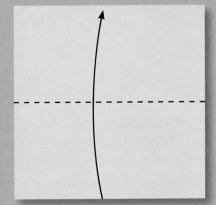

## Valley fold
The paper is folded forward, making a crease at the bottom.

## Mountain fold
The paper is folded behind, making a crease at the top.

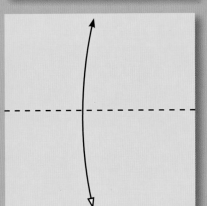

## Crease and unfold
Here, you make a standard valley fold, starting at the hollow arrowhead and folding to the solid arrowhead. Make a firm crease, then unfold.

# Origami paper

Origami requires paper that is perfectly square, and thin enough to crease easily without cracking. There are 50 sheets of patterned paper in the pack, plus two sheets of waterproof paper, and one sheet of foil paper.

## Choosing paper

Choose a pattern that suits the final design.

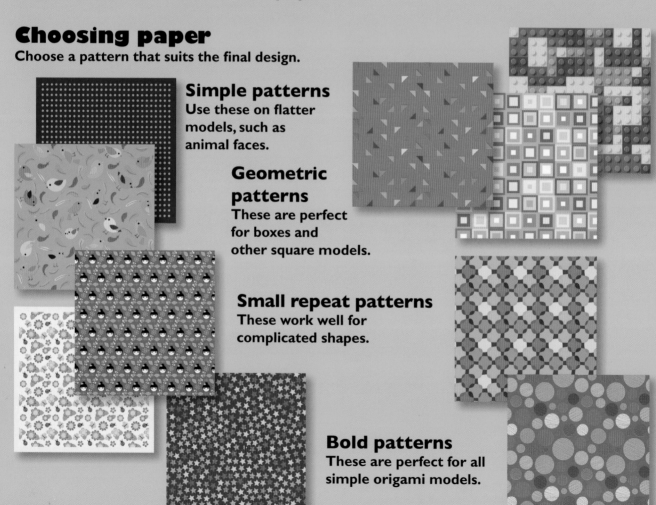

### Simple patterns
Use these on flatter models, such as animal faces.

### Geometric patterns
These are perfect for boxes and other square models.

### Small repeat patterns
These work well for complicated shapes.

### Bold patterns
These are perfect for all simple origami models.

## Using different papers

You can make all the models in the pack using the paper supplied, or try making them with your own paper. You can make them bigger or smaller, as long as you always start with a perfect square. Try using sheets of wrapping paper for really big models—just cut it into squares, and follow the instructions as before.

## Waterproof paper

Use the waterproof paper from the pack for any of the aquatic origami models, or the origami cup. Greaseproof paper can also make good water-resistant models.

## Foil paper

Foil paper can be quite tricky to work with. It creases easily where you don't want it to! Some foil papers can also split easily. Try experimenting with foil wrapping paper.

# Create a perfect square

Here is a simple method for creating a square from a rectangle. The paper should be crisp and capable of "remembering" a crease (so it doesn't try to unfold itself).

Use this technique to create large squares of origami paper from wrapping paper, newspaper, or greaseproof paper to create really big models.

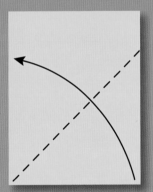

Fold a short edge to a long edge.

Fold the surplus paper over the edge, crease, and unfold.

Unfold the paper fully.

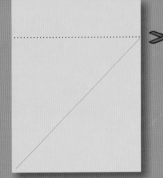

Cut off the excess paper to leave a square. Can you invent a model using the leftover paper?

# Bases

Here are some simple techniques you should practice before starting the models in this book.

## Preliminary base

**1** Patterned side up, fold in half from corner to opposite corner, crease, and unfold, in both directions.

**2**

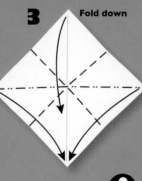

Crease
Crease

**3** Fold the paper downward using only these three creases.

**1**

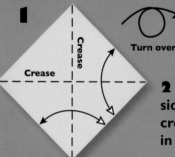

Crease

Crease

**Turn over**

**2** Fold in half from side to opposite side, crease, and unfold, in both directions.

**3**

**Fold down**

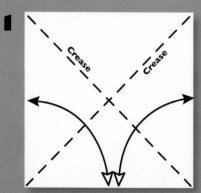

The preliminary base

> ! The preliminary base is used in the box, star box, and four-pointed star models.

## Blintz base

**1**

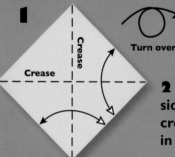

Crease    Crease

**1** Plain side up, fold in half from corner to opposite corner, crease and unfold, in both directions.

**2**

Fold in          Fold in

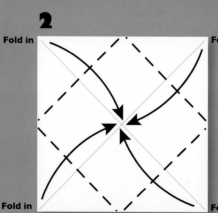

Fold in          Fold in

**2** Fold all four corners to the center of the paper.

The Blintz base

> ! The name "Blintz" comes from a type of pastry. It is used in the fortune teller, Masu box, and crown models.

# Outside reverse fold

**Start with a square folded on a diagonal.**

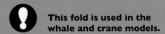

This fold is used in the whale and crane models.

**1**

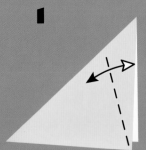

**2**

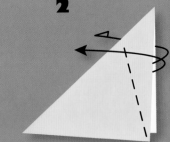

**3**

**3** This is the fold in progress.

**1** Fold the right edge over (the angle isn't important), crease, and unfold.

**2** Wrap the paper around the outside—the valley crease shown is the same on the layer underneath.

The completed fold

# Inside reverse fold

**Start with a square folded on a diagonal.**

This fold is used in the swan and peacock models.

**1**

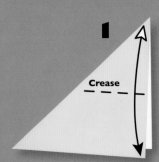

Crease

**2**

Push in

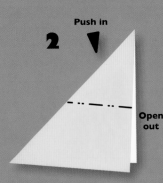

Open out

**3**

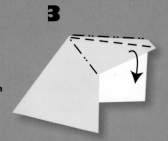

The completed fold

**1** Fold the end of a diagonal fold down to the corner, crease, and unfold.

**2** Push the corner inside. Open the layers to allow this.

**3** The fold in progress—no new creases are needed!

The completed fold

9

# Fan

This classic origami design is full of symbolism. The handle represents the beginning of life and the folds represent the roads of life spreading to bring good fortune and happiness.

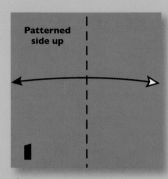

**Patterned side up**

**1**

**1** Patterned side up, crease in half from side to side, then unfold.

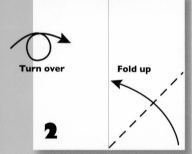

**Turn over**      **Fold up**

**2**

**2** Fold the lower right corner up to the vertical crease.

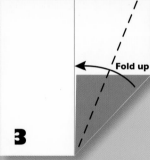

**Fold up**

**3**

**3** Take the folded edge to the vertical crease.

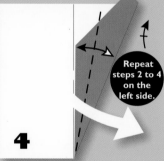

**Repeat steps 2 to 4 on the left side.**

**4**

**4** Take the folded edge to the vertical crease, and unfold completely.

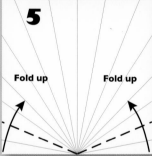

**5**

**Fold up**      **Fold up**

**5** Refold on existing creases to where the arrows are pointing.

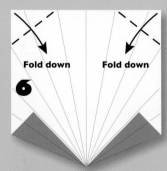

**Fold down**      **Fold down**

**6**

**6** Fold down the upper corners in between the ends of the creases.

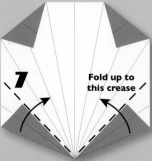

**7**

**Fold up to this crease**

**7** Refold on existing creases to where the arrows are pointing.

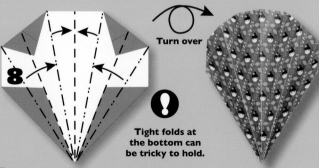

**8**

**Turn over**

**Tight folds at the bottom can be tricky to hold.**

**8** Make the above alternating valley and mountain folds. Turn the paper over and partially unfold.

**The finished fan**

10

# ■Bookmark

This useful model is very easy to fold.
Make bookmarks in a variety of papers—
they will make perfect gifts!

**1**

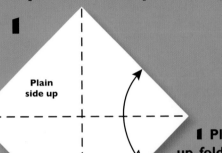

Plain
side up

**1** Plain side
up, fold corner
to opposite corner,
crease, and unfold,
in both directions.

**2**

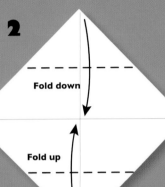

Fold down

Fold up

**2** Fold
upper
and lower
corners to
the center.

**3**

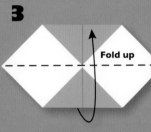

Fold up

**3** Fold in half upward.

**4**

Fold in

**4** Fold half of the
lower (folded) edge
to the vertical
center crease.

**5**

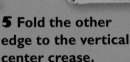

Fold in

**5** Fold the other
edge to the vertical
center crease.

**6**

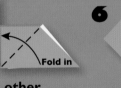

**6** This is how it
should look.

Turn over

**7**

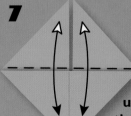

**7** Fold the
upper corners to
the bottom corner,
crease firmly, and unfold.

**8**

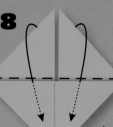

**8** Refold
the flaps,
tucking them
into a pocket.

The finished
bookmark

11

# Fortune teller

This model is also known as a chatterbox. It is a great way to practice accurate folding.

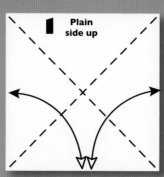

**1** Plain side up, fold corner to opposite corner, crease, and unfold, in both directions.

**2** Fold all four corners to the center.

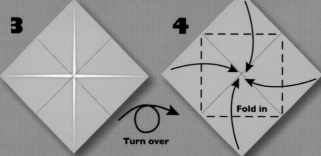

**3** This is how it should look.

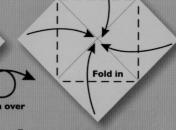

**4** Again, fold all four corners to the center.

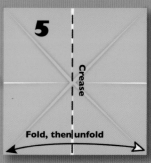

**5** Fold in half from side to side, crease, and unfold.

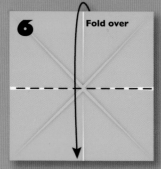

**6** Fold in half downward.

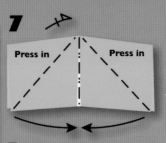

**7** Press the short sides together, allowing the paper to open on the creases shown, both front and back.

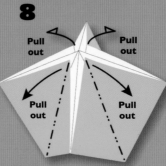

**8** Carefully peel open the four corners.

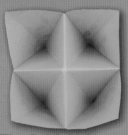

The finished fortune teller. Turn to page 48 for instructions on how to use it as a fortune teller.

# Cup

You can make this cup from origami paper and it will be strong enough to drink from, or use the waterproof paper from the pack for a really strong cup.

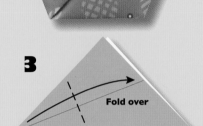

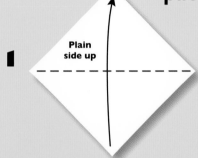

**1** Plain side up, fold corner to opposite corner.

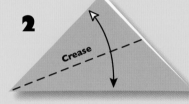

**2** Fold a single upper left edge to lie on the lower (folded) edge, crease, and unfold.

**3** Fold the lower left corner to touch the end of the last crease you made.

**4** Fold a single triangular flap over the edges, crease, and unfold.

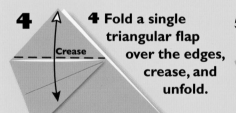

**5** Refold a single flap, tucking it into a pocket.

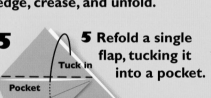

**6** This is how it should look.

Turn over

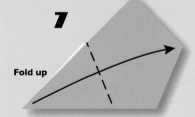

**7** Fold the lower left corner to touch the right corner.

**8** Fold the triangular flap over the edges, crease, and unfold.

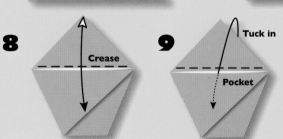

**9** Refold the flap, tucking it into a pocket.

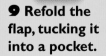

The finished cup

# ■ Wallet

Using paper from the pack, this wallet is perfect for small items such as stamps. To make a wallet suitable for business or credit cards, start with a 9-inch square sheet of paper.

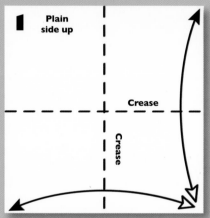

**1** Plain side up, fold side to opposite side, crease, and unfold, in both directions.

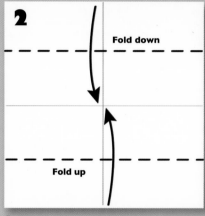

**2** Fold upper and lower edges to the horizontal center.

**3** This is how it should look.

Turn over

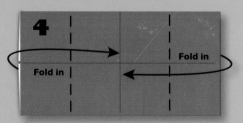

**4** Fold left and right edges to the vertical center.

**5** Fold in half downward.

The finished wallet

# Boat

This is a model of a traditional Japanese fishing boat. Make it using any of the papers in the pack, but if you use the waterproof paper, your boat will last much longer. Try making bigger boats with greaseproof paper, which also floats well.

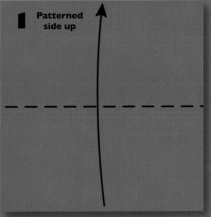

**1** Patterned side up

**1** Patterned side up, fold in half upward.

Turn over

**2**

Fold

**2** Fold both upper edges to the lower edge.

**3**

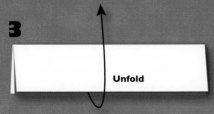

Unfold

**3** Unfold a single layer.

**4**

**4** This is how it should look.

**5**

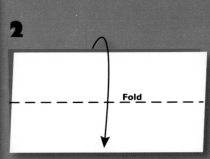

Fold in     Fold in

Fold in     Fold in

**5** Fold all four corners (two will have more than one layer) to lie on the horizontal center crease.

**6**

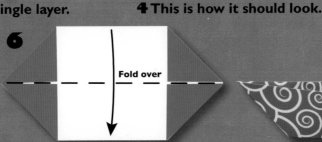

Fold over

**6** Fold in half downward.

The finished boat

# Sailboat

The classic sailboat is the symbol of the Origami USA group. You can vary the shape of the smaller sail by adjusting the distance of the gap in step 8. Using the paper from the pack, this model will measure 3½ inches tall. Once you've mastered the technique, try making a whole fleet of boats in different papers and sizes.

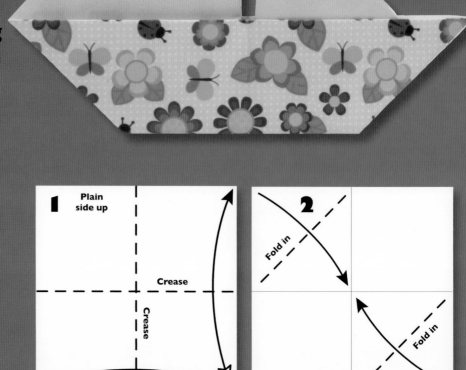

**1** Plain side up

Crease

Crease

**2** Fold in

Fold in

Fold in

**1** Plain side up, fold side to opposite side, crease, and unfold, in both directions.

**2** Fold opposite corners to the center.

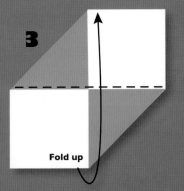

**3** Fold in half upward.

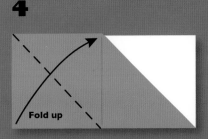

**4** Fold the lower left corner to the center of the upper edge.

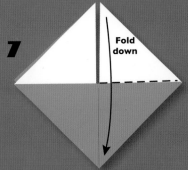

**5** Fold the lower right corner behind in the same way.

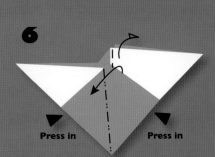

**6** Gently press the outer edges together, allowing the layers to squash open in the opposite direction.

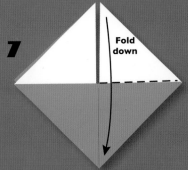

**7** Fold the upper right flap to the lower corner.

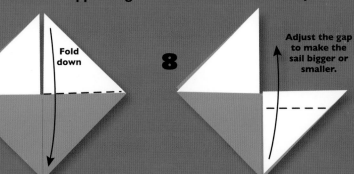

**8** Leaving a small gap, fold the same flap back upward.

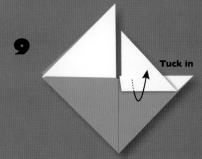

**9** Ease out the flap and tuck the white edge inside the pocket.

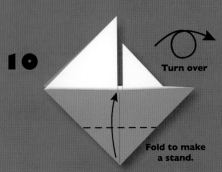

**10** Fold the lower corner to the center, then open out at 90 degrees to form a stand.

The finished sailboat

# ⊠ Fish

The fish symbolizes happiness and freedom. Choose paper with a scaly pattern, or make it with waterproof paper.

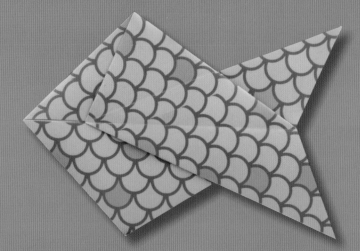

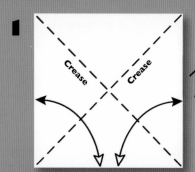

**1** Plain side up, fold corner to opposite corner, crease, and unfold, in both directions.

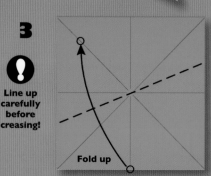

**2** Fold side to opposite side, crease, and unfold, in both directions.

**3** Fold so that the lower center point lies on the upper diagonal crease, with the fold passing through the center of the paper.

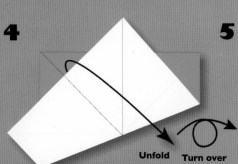

**4** Unfold the last fold.

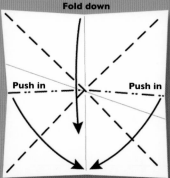

**5** Push the paper down using existing creases to form a triangle.

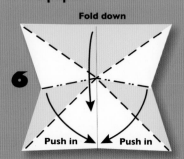

**6** This is what the paper will look like as you fold it down.

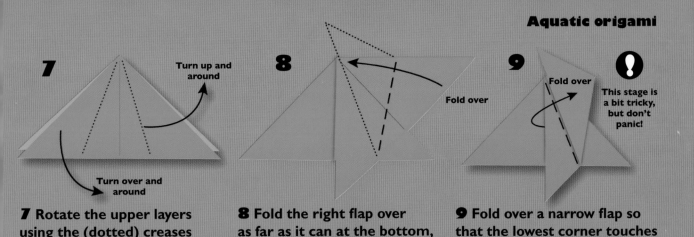

**7** Rotate the upper layers using the (dotted) creases inside the paper.

**8** Fold the right flap over as far as it can at the bottom, so it passes through the top corner.

**9** Fold over a narrow flap so that the lowest corner touches the corner on the right.

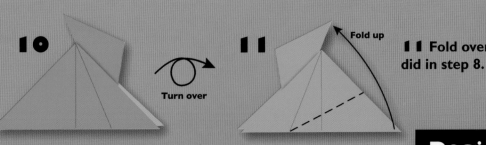

**10** This is how it should look. Turn the paper over.

**11** Fold over as you did in step 8.

## Design ideas

**1** Decorate the scales with dots of glitter.
**2** Make a gold fish by using the foil paper from your pack.

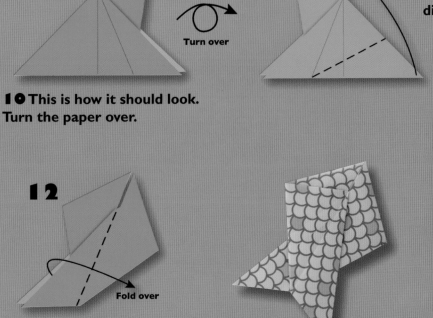

**12** Fold over a narrow flap.

**The finished fish**

# Whale

An old and much-loved origami design based on our biggest mammal. You can make the tail fin larger by adjusting the crease in step 11.

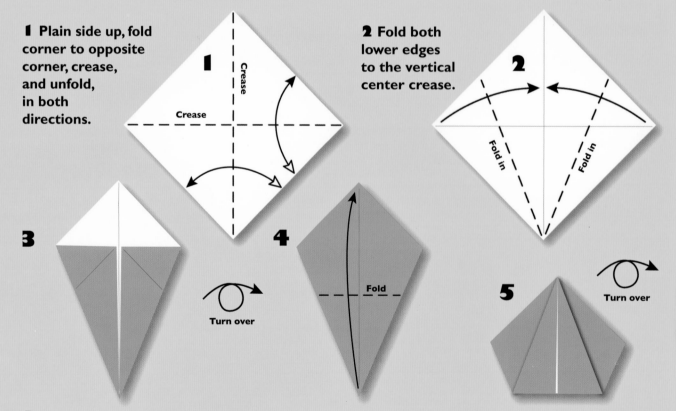

**1** Plain side up, fold corner to opposite corner, crease, and unfold, in both directions.

**1**

Crease

Crease

**2** Fold both lower edges to the vertical center crease.

**2**

Fold in

Fold in

**3**

Turn over

**4**

Fold

**5**

Turn over

**3** This is how it should look.

**4** Fold the lower corner to the top corner.

**5** This is how it should look.

**6**

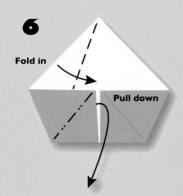

Fold in

Pull down

**6** Pull down the left colored corner, folding in the side at the same time.

**7**

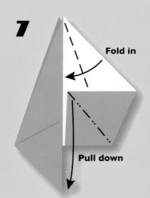

Fold in

Pull down

**7** Repeat the last step on the right.

**8**

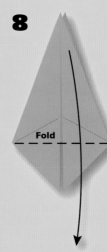

Fold

**8** Fold the upper layer downward and rotate the paper 90 degrees counter-clockwise.

**9**

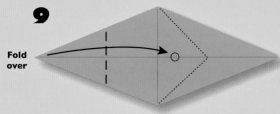

Fold over

**9** Fold the left corner to the circled point.

**10**

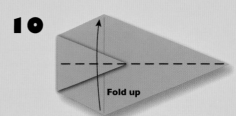

Fold up

**10** Fold in half upward.

**11**

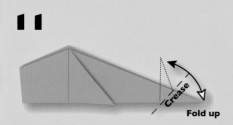

Crease

Fold up

**11** Fold the tail upward, crease, and unfold.

**12**

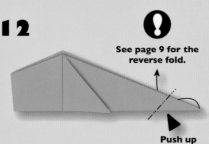

See page 9 for the reverse fold.

Push up

**12** Push the tail upward between the layers, making a reverse fold.

The finished whale

# Water bomb

This design, also know as a water balloon, is unusual as it needs to be inflated to create the final shape. It can be filled with water, or just inflated with air, to make a pretty hanging decoration.

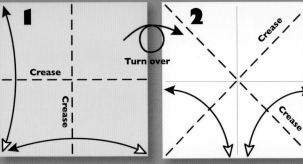

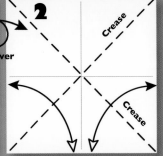

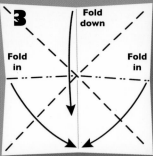

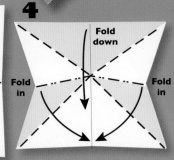

**1** Patterned side up, fold side to opposite side, crease, and unfold, in both directions.

**2** Fold corner to opposite corner, crease, and unfold, in both directions.

**3** Fold the paper down using the existing creases.

**4** This is how the paper will look halfway through step 3, as you fold it down to form a triangle.

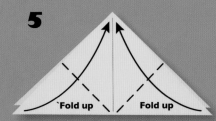

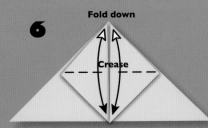

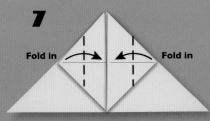

**5** Fold outer corners to the top corner, on the upper layers only.

**6** Fold upper corners to the lower corner, crease, and unfold.

**7** Fold corners on the left and right to the center.

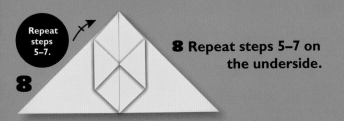

**Repeat steps 5–7.**

**8** Repeat steps 5–7 on the underside.

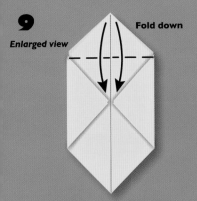

*Enlarged view*

Fold down

**9** Fold down two corners to the center.

Crease  Crease

**10** Fold two triangular flaps over edges, crease, and unfold.

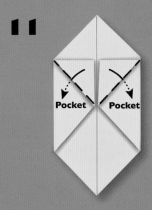

Pocket  Pocket

**11** Refold both flaps, tucking them into pockets.

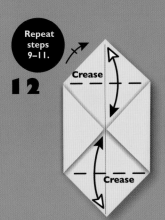

**Repeat steps 9–11.**

Crease

Crease

**12** Repeat steps 9–11 on the underside. Fold upper and lower corners to the center, crease, and unfold.

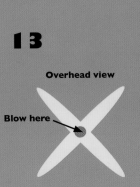

Overhead view

Blow here

**13** If you open the model out a little and look at one end overhead, it will look like this, with a hole.

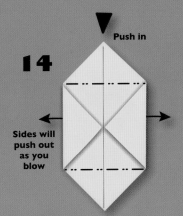

Push in

Sides will push out as you blow

**14** Blow into the hole in the corner, encouraging the paper to open out into a three-dimensional shape.

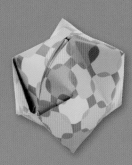

The finished water bomb

# Menko

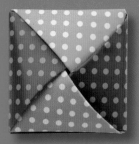

This traditional Menko model derives from a Japanese card game. The model is unusual as it uses two contrasting sheets of paper.

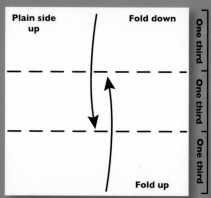

Plain side up     Fold down

One third

One third

One third

Fold up

**1** With your first sheet of paper, plain side up, fold the edges in so they overlap as closely as possible.

## 2

Fold    Fold

**2** Fold opposite corners over.

## 3

Crease    Crease

**3** Fold corner to corner, crease, and unfold, on both sides.

## 4

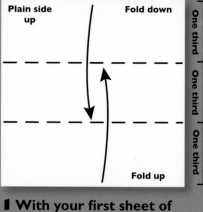

**4** With your second sheet, repeat steps 1–3. Arrange as shown and fold a flap over.

## 5

**5** Fold the lower flap upward.

Fold up

## 6

Fold across

**6** Fold the left flap to the right.

## 7

Fold down

Tuck in here

**7** Fold the top flap down, tucking it behind the right-hand pocket.

**!** Take care when tucking in—it can be tight.

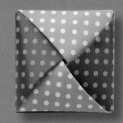

The finished Menko model. Turn to page 48 for instructions on how to play the game.

# Purse

Using paper from the pack, this purse is perfect for keeping stamps and small notes in.

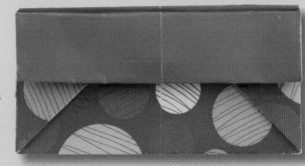

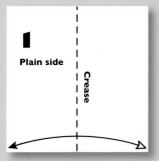

**1** Plain side up, fold side to opposite side, crease, and unfold.

**2** Fold in half upward.

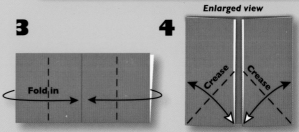

**3** Fold left and right edges to the vertical center.

**4** Fold the lower inside corners to the outer edges, crease, and unfold.

*Enlarged view*

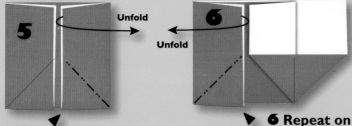

**5** Unfold a single layer to the right, carefully flattening the lower corner into a triangle.

**6** Repeat on the left.

**7** Fold the outer sections behind.

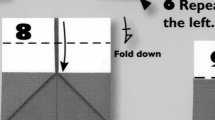

**8** Fold the white section in half downward. Repeat on the other side.

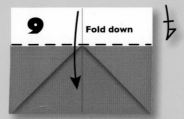

**9** Fold the white section over again. Repeat behind.

The finished purse

# Envelope

Using paper from your pack, you can make a small envelope, but if you make it with a larger sheet of paper, it will be big enough to use for a greeting card.

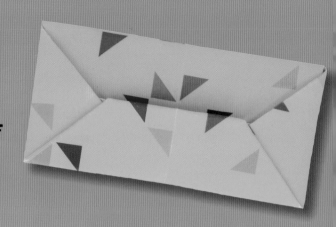

**1** Plain side up, fold side to opposite side, crease, and unfold.

**2** Fold left and right edges to the vertical center, crease, and unfold.

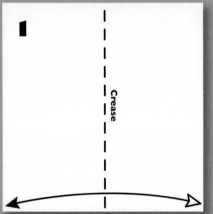

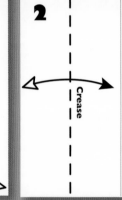

**3** Fold in half upward.

**4** Fold the paper in half upward, crease, and unfold.

**5** Fold a single layer down to the center crease.

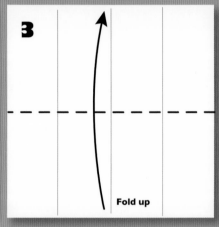

**6** Fold two small corners over.

26

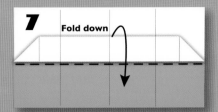

**7** Fold the white flap downward.

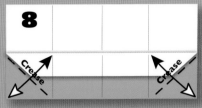

**8** Fold the corners inward, crease, and unfold.

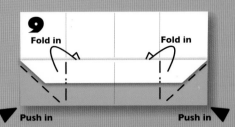

**9** Tuck the white flap inside. Push the bottom corners inward.

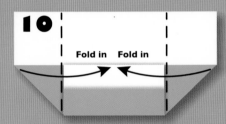

**10** Fold the sides inward as much as possible—the layers may be thick.

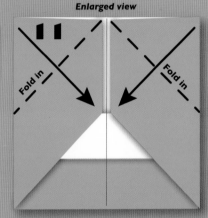

*Enlarged view*

**11** Fold the top corners to the center.

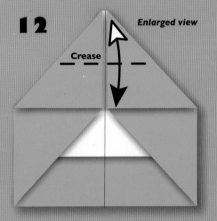

*Enlarged view*

**12** Fold the top corner to the center, crease, and unfold.

**Fold firmly through thick layers.**

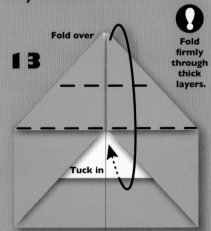

**13** Using the two creases shown, fold the corner down and tuck it under a flap.

The finished envelope

27

# ⊠ Masu box

In ancient Japan, masu boxes were square wooden boxes, made in different sizes, which were used to measure rice.

This model is strong, but simple to make. Using paper from your pack, the box will measure about 2½ inches wide. Once you've mastered the technique for this box, try making a stack of boxes in different colors and sizes.

❗ This needs careful, sharp folds for a good result.

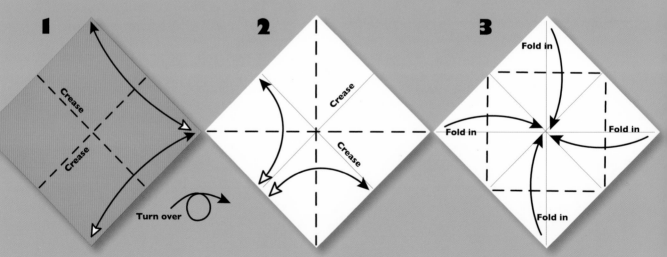

**1** Patterned side up, fold side to opposite side, crease, and unfold, in both directions.

**2** Fold corner to opposite corner, crease, and unfold, in both directions.

**3** Fold all four corners to the center.

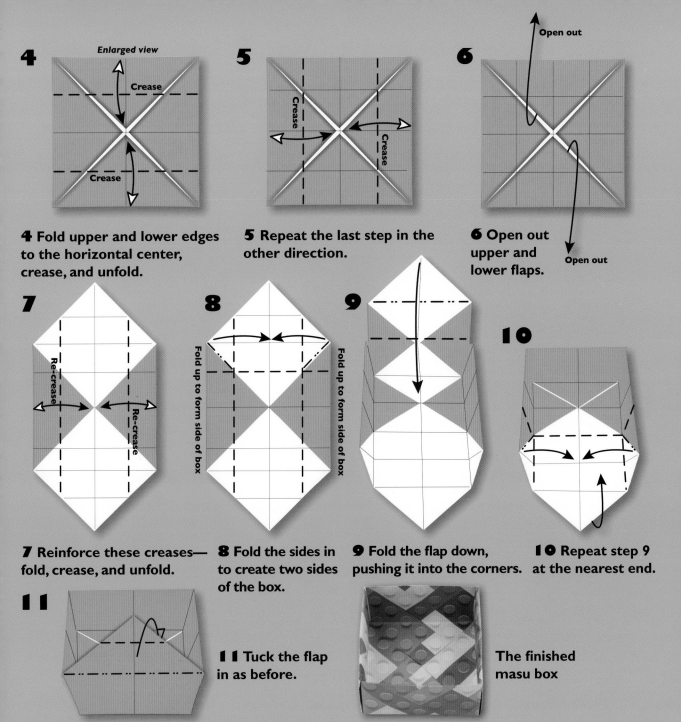

**4** Fold upper and lower edges to the horizontal center, crease, and unfold.

**5** Repeat the last step in the other direction.

**6** Open out upper and lower flaps.

**7** Reinforce these creases—fold, crease, and unfold.

**8** Fold the sides in to create two sides of the box.

**9** Fold the flap down, pushing it into the corners.

**10** Repeat step 9 at the nearest end.

**11** Tuck the flap in as before.

The finished masu box

# Box

There are three origami boxes in this book. This design has a clever built-in lid. Using the paper in your pack, your box will measure nearly 2½ inches wide. Try making it in different sizes to store all your stuff!

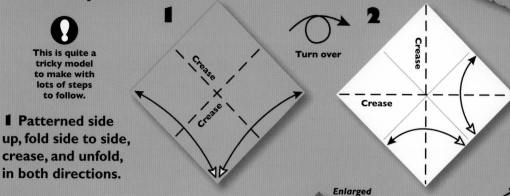

**!** This is quite a tricky model to make with lots of steps to follow.

**1** Patterned side up, fold side to side, crease, and unfold, in both directions.

**1**

Crease
Crease

**Turn over**

**2**

Crease
Crease

**2** Fold corner to opposite corner, crease, and unfold, in both directions.

**3**

Fold in        Fold in

Fold up

**3** Fold the paper up using these creases to create a square.

**4**

*Enlarged view*

**4** Make a small pinch to mark the center of the paper.

**5**

Fold in

Fold in        Fold in

**5** Fold the corners of the three uppermost layers to the center. Repeat underneath.

**6**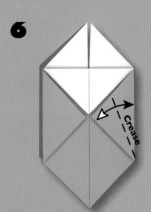

**6** Fold the inner edge to the outer edge, crease, and unfold.

**7**

**7** Open and squash the right-hand flap into a kite shape.

**8**

**8** Repeat steps 6 and 7 on the left-hand flap and (twice) underneath.

**9**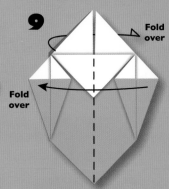

**9** Fold a flap from right to left and repeat underneath.

**10**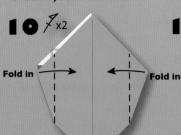

Fold in        Fold in

**10** Fold in twice on existing creases. Repeat underneath.

**11**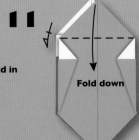

Fold down

Fold down

**11** Fold the top corner to the center. Repeat underneath.

**12** Fold down

**12** Fold the white flap downward. Repeat underneath.

**13**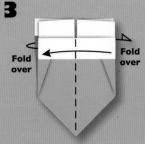

Fold over        Fold over

**13** Fold a flap from right to left and repeat underneath.

**14**

Fold down

**14** Fold the white flap downward. Repeat underneath.

**15**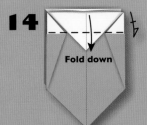

Crease

**15** Make a crease connecting the two lower corners, crease and unfold.

**16**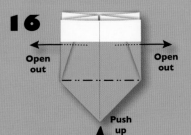

Open out        Open out

Push up

**16** Open the model from inside, forming the box. Sharpen all corners.

The finished box

# Frame

Using paper from your pack, your frame will measure about 3 inches wide—perfect for a small photograph. Once you've learned the technique, try making a frame with metallic paper.

**1** Plain side up, fold corner to opposite corner, crease, and unfold, in both directions.

**I**
Plain side
Crease
Crease

**2**
Crease

**3**
Fold up

**2** Fold the lower corner to the center, crease, and unfold.

**3** Fold the lower corner to the nearest crease.

**4**
Fold up

**4** Fold the colored triangle in half upward.

**5**
Fold up

**5** Fold the colored area upward.

Repeat steps 2–5.

**6**

**6** This is how it should look. Repeat steps 2–5 on the three remaining corners.

**7**
Turn over

**7** This is the result.

**8**
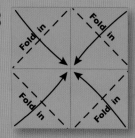
Fold in · Fold in · Fold in · Fold in

**8** Fold all four corners to the center. Rotate the paper 90 degrees.

**9**
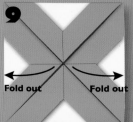
Fold out · Fold out

**9** Open two flaps out halfway to become stands. Turn over and add your photo!

Turn over

The finished frame

# Crown

Using the paper from your pack, this makes a perfect decoration. If you use a sheet of paper 16 inches square, it will be big enough to wear!

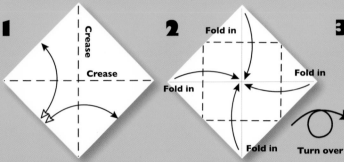

**1**

**1** Plain side up, fold corner to opposite corner, crease, and unfold, in both directions.

**2**

**2** Fold all four corners to the center.

**Turn over**

**3**

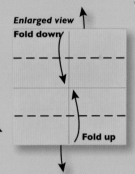

*Enlarged view*
**Fold down**

**Fold up**

**3** Fold upper and lower edges to the horizontal center, allowing corners to "flip out" from underneath.

Use foil paper from your pack to make a shiny crown decoration.

**4**

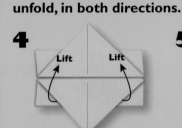

Lift   Lift

**4** Lift a single layer upward.

**5**

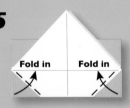

Fold in   Fold in

**5** Fold the lower triangular flaps to the halfway crease.

**6**

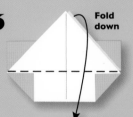

Fold down

**6** Fold two layers downward.

**7**

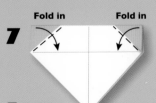

Fold in   Fold in

**7** Fold down the upper triangular flaps.

**8**

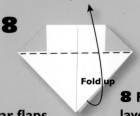

Fold up

**8** Fold a single layer upward.

**9**

Open out

**9** Open the model from within and shape into a crown. You can leave the short edges rounded or sharpen into a crease.

# Star box

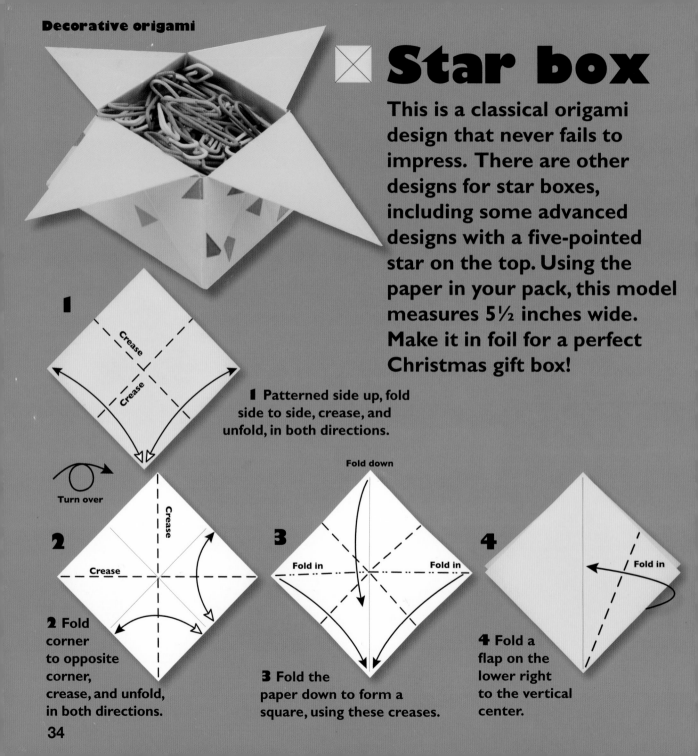

This is a classical origami design that never fails to impress. There are other designs for star boxes, including some advanced designs with a five-pointed star on the top. Using the paper in your pack, this model measures 5½ inches wide. Make it in foil for a perfect Christmas gift box!

**1**

Crease

Crease

**1** Patterned side up, fold side to side, crease, and unfold, in both directions.

Turn over

**2**

Crease

Crease

**2** Fold corner to opposite corner, crease, and unfold, in both directions.

**3**

Fold down

Fold in    Fold in

**3** Fold the paper down to form a square, using these creases.

**4**

Fold in

**4** Fold a flap on the lower right to the vertical center.

34

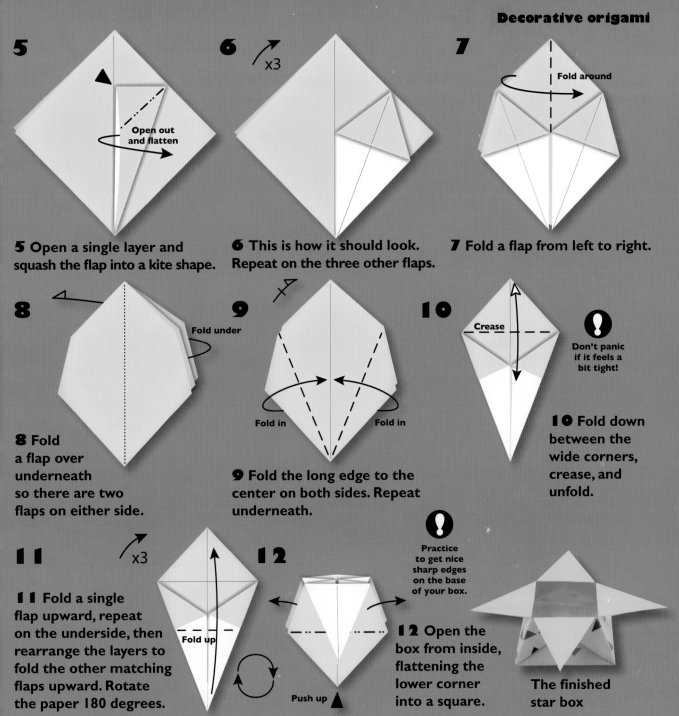

**5** Open a single layer and squash the flap into a kite shape.

Open out and flatten

**6** This is how it should look. Repeat on the three other flaps.

x3

**7** Fold a flap from left to right.

Fold around

**8** Fold a flap over underneath so there are two flaps on either side.

Fold under

**9** Fold the long edge to the center on both sides. Repeat underneath.

Fold in    Fold in

**10** Fold down between the wide corners, crease, and unfold.

Crease

Don't panic if it feels a bit tight!

**11** Fold a single flap upward, repeat on the underside, then rearrange the layers to fold the other matching flaps upward. Rotate the paper 180 degrees.

x3

Fold up

**12** Open the box from inside, flattening the lower corner into a square.

Push up

Practice to get nice sharp edges on the base of your box.

The finished star box

35

# Four-pointed star

The four-pointed star is sometimes known as the Star of Bethlehem. It may be easier to try making it with a larger square of paper than the paper from your pack.

This is probably the most challenging model in the book! You will need to fold carefully and neatly to make good sharp points.

**1**

**1** Plain side up, fold corner to opposite corner, crease, and unfold, in both directions.

**2** x3

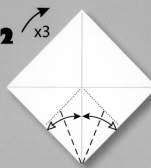

**2** Fold each lower edge to the vertical center, creasing only to the (imaginary) dotted lines above, then unfold.

Turn over

**3**

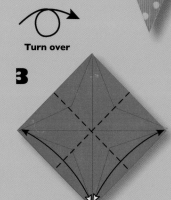

**3** Fold side to side, crease, and unfold, in both directions.

Fold down

**4**

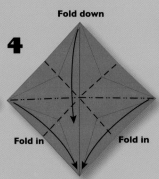

Fold in        Fold in

**4** Fold the paper down to form a square using these creases.

**5**        Enlarged view

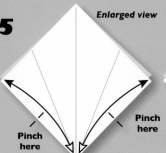

Pinch here        Pinch here

**5** Fold the lower corner to the outer corners, make a pinch at the halfway point, and unfold.

**6**

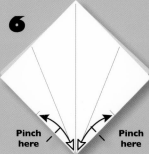

Pinch here        Pinch here

**6** Fold the lower corners to the recent pinches. Make another firm pinch then unfold.

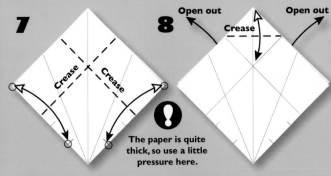

**7**

Crease ┼ Crease

The paper is quite thick, so use a little pressure here.

**7** Fold the outer corners to the most recent pinches, so the circled points meet, crease firmly through all layers and unfold.

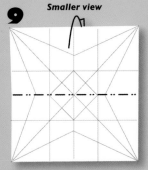

**8** Open out — Crease — Open out

**8** Fold the top corner to the nearest creases, crease, and unfold. Open the layers from underneath.

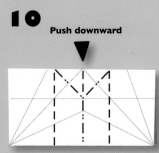

**9** Smaller view

**9** Fold the top half behind.

**10** Push downward

**10** Press down in the center of the top edge, forming a pleat along the mountain crease.

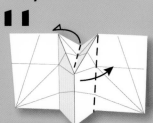

**11**

**11** Fold the central flap to the right, folding the matching flap underneath in the opposite direction.

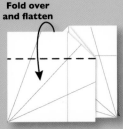

**12** Fold over and flatten

**12** Well done! Fold a flap downward.

**13**

Turn over

**13** This is how it should look.

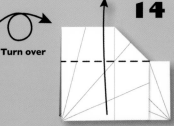

**14**

**14** Fold a flap upward.

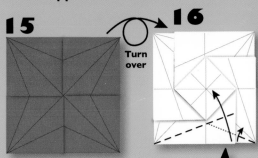

**15**

Turn over

**15** This is how it should look.

**16**

**16** Fold over on the long valley crease. As you do so, fold up the similar valley crease that is revealed. As the layers fold toward the center, flatten into a new crease.

**17**

**17** Repeat on the next side, counter-clockwise.

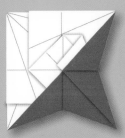

**18**

x2

**18** This is how it should look. Repeat on the other two sides, tucking the last flap under the first to lock it together.

37

# Owl

The owl is a symbol of good luck and happiness in Japan. Draw or stick on the eyes. If you use plain paper, you can draw feathers on your owl as well.

**1**

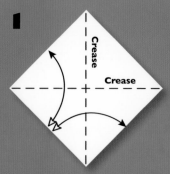

**1** Plain side up, fold corner to opposite corner, crease, and unfold, in both directions.

**2**

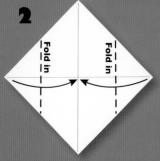

**2** Fold left and right corners to the center.

**3**

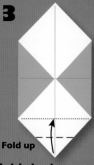

**3** Fold the lower corner to the (imaginary) dotted line (above).

**4**

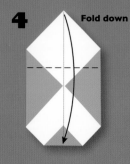

**4** Fold the top corner to the bottom edge.

**5**

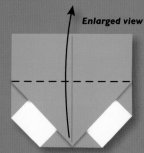

**5** Fold a flap upward between the corners.

**6**

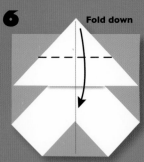

**6** Fold the corner down to form the eyes and beak.

**7**

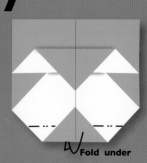

**7** Fold the lower section underneath.

**8**

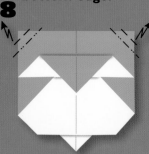

**8** Make pleats by folding the top corners one way then the other to form ears.

**The finished owl**

When you've finished the model, add some eyes to make your owl come to life.

38

# ■ Puppy

Play around with the position of the eyes and nose to change the expression on this simple model.

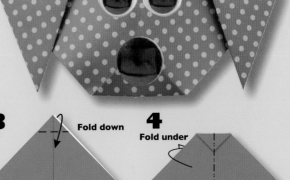

**1**

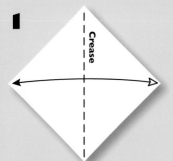

Crease

**1** Plain side up, fold from the right corner to the left corner, crease, and unfold.

**2**

Fold up

**2** Fold in half upward.

**3**

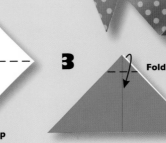

Fold down

**3** Fold two flaps over at the top to form the nose.

**4**

Fold under

**4** Fold the left half behind

**5**

Fold up to here

**5** Fold a layer up to match the dotted line.

**6**

Turn over

**6** This is how it should look.

**7**

Fold up again

**7** Fold the flap up to match the one underneath.

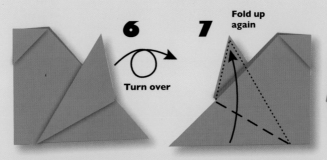

**8**

Turn over

Unfold

**8** Open out the lower half.

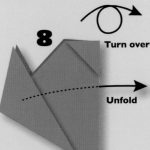

**9**

Rotate

**9** Turn the model around.

The finished puppy. When you've finished the model, draw on a shiny nose and stick on, or draw the eyes.

# Butterfly

The butterfly symbolizes change, love, and joy. Make lots of bright butterflies and hang them around your home to create a sense of well-being. Take your time and fold carefully to create this beautiful model.

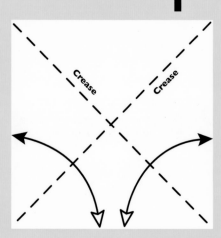

**1** Plain side up, fold corner to opposite corner, crease, and unfold, in both directions.

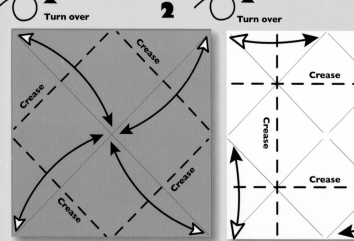

**2** Fold all four corners to the center, crease, and unfold.

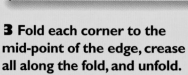

**3** Fold each corner to the mid-point of the edge, crease all along the fold, and unfold.

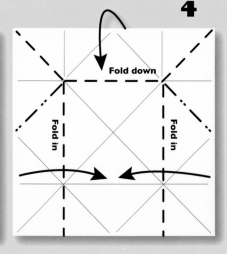

**4** Fold the sides in and the top down, using these (existing) creases.

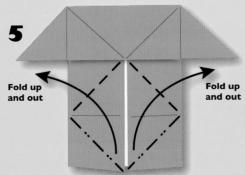

**5**

Fold up and out

Fold up and out

**5** This is how it should look. Lift the lower colored corners up and outward, repeating the last step.

**6**

Fold over

**6** Fold the upper half behind.

**7**

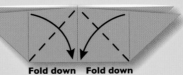

Fold down    Fold down

**7** Fold a single flap down on either side so the edges are vertical.

**8**

Fold in    Fold in

**8** Fold the sides in at a slight angle.

**9**

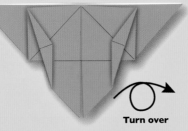

Turn over

**9** This is how it should look.

**10**

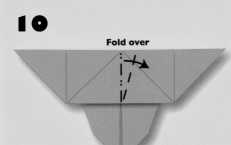

Fold over

**10** Fold the left half of the model over to the right at a slight angle.

**11**

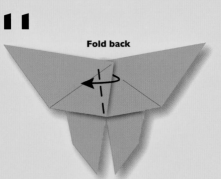

Fold back

**11** Fold the central flap to the left, then open to half way.

The finished butterfly

41

# ⊠ Swan

Swans are a symbol of love and faithfulness, and origami swans are used as decorations at wedding celebrations. This model needs extra care when folding, but the results are worth it!

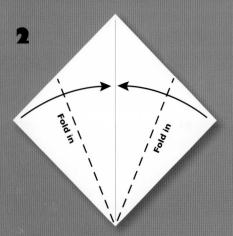

❗ Fold carefully and neatly to obtain the clean lines of a real swan.

**1**

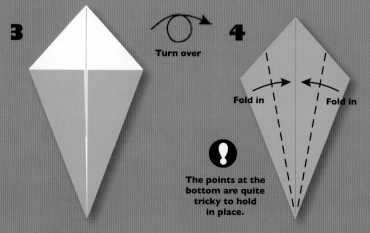

Crease

**1** Plain side up, fold from the right corner to left corner, crease, and unfold.

**2**

Fold in — Fold in

**2** Fold the lower edges to the vertical center.

**3**

**3** This is how it should look.

Turn over

**4**

Fold in — Fold in

❗ The points at the bottom are quite tricky to hold in place.

**4** Fold the long edges to the vertical center.

**5**

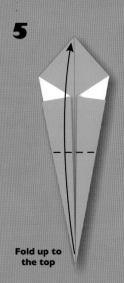

Fold up to
the top

**5** Fold the lower corner
to the top corner.

**6**

Fold back

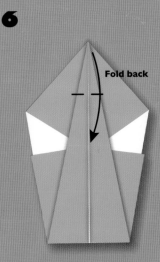

**6** Fold back a short flap to
form the beak.

**7**

Fold under

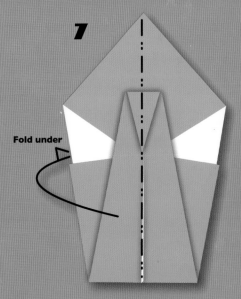

**7** Fold the left half of the
model underneath.

**8**

Ease out

Rotate

Hold
here

Hold here

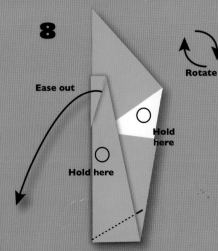

**8** Hold the circled areas and
ease the neck out, flattening
when it is in position.

Pull up and out

**9**

**!** Take care when
you pull out the
paper to create
the beak.

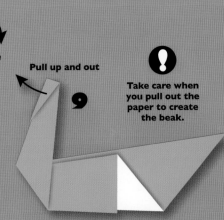

**9** Pull out the beak and
flatten into position.

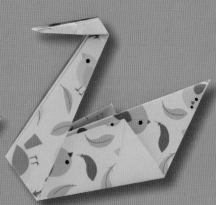

The finished swan

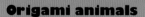

**Look out for some tricky folds when making this model.**

# Peacock

The peacock is a symbol of compassion and kindness, and it is thought to promote good health. It's quite a tricky model to make, so take your time!

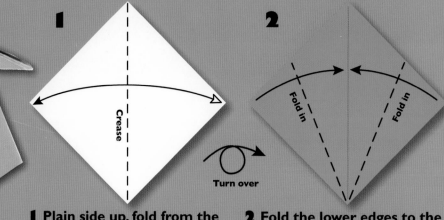

**1**

Crease

Turn over

**1** Plain side up, fold from the right corner to left corner, crease, and unfold.

**2**

Fold in   Fold in

**2** Fold the lower edges to the vertical center.

**3**

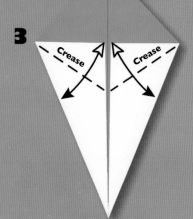

Crease   Crease

**3** Fold the short plain edges to the outside edge, crease, and unfold.

**4**

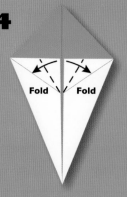

Fold   Fold

**4** Fold the plain edges to the recent crease on both sides.

**5**

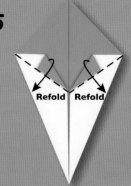

Refold   Refold

**5** Refold the two edges using the creases from step 3.

**6**

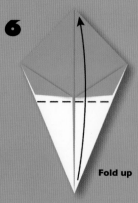

Fold up

**6** Fold up the lower corner to the top corner.

**7**

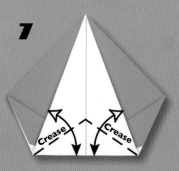

**7** Fold each side of the plain flap to the lower edge, creasing to the center only, then unfolding.

**8**

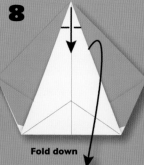

Fold down

**8** Fold the top corner down a little way, then fold the plain flap downward.

**9** Fold the flap over at a right angle to the lower right edge, so the lower left edge touches the end of the crease.

**9**

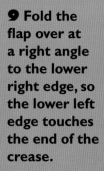

Crease

**10**

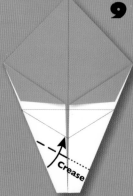

9-10

Unfold

**10** Unfold the flap and repeat the last step on the other side.

Don't panic at this stage!

**11**

**11** Start to put in these creases, forming a three-dimensional shape. Make no new creases and check the next step!

Fold back

**12**

Front view

Fold back          Fold back

**12** Here is the move in progress.

**13**

**13** Fold a single layer at the back of the tail to the vertical edge.

13-14

**14**

Repeat steps 13-14.

**14** Fold the new flap in half. Repeat steps 13–14 on the underside.

**15**

Lift out carefully

**15** Lift up and flatten the beak. Partially unfold the tail feathers.

The finished peacock

# Crane

The crane is the well-known symbol of peace. People in Japan like to fold 1,000 of these as a symbol of long life. This model takes some practice.

**Don't panic!** You will need to fold this several times to perfect it.

**1**

Crease

Crease

**1** Patterned side up, fold corner to opposite corner, crease, and unfold.

Turn over

**2**

Crease

Crease

**2** Fold side to side, crease, and unfold, in both directions.

**3**

Fold down

Fold in     Fold in

**3** Fold the paper down to form a square using these creases.

**4**

Enlarged view

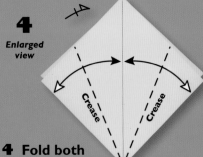

Crease    Crease

**4** Fold both lower flaps to the vertical center, crease, and unfold. Repeat underneath.

**5**

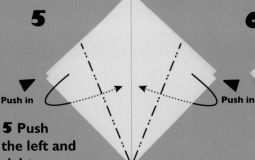

Push in        Push in

**5** Push the left and right corners inside the layers, making reverse folds.

**6**

**6** This is how it should look. Repeat the last step underneath.

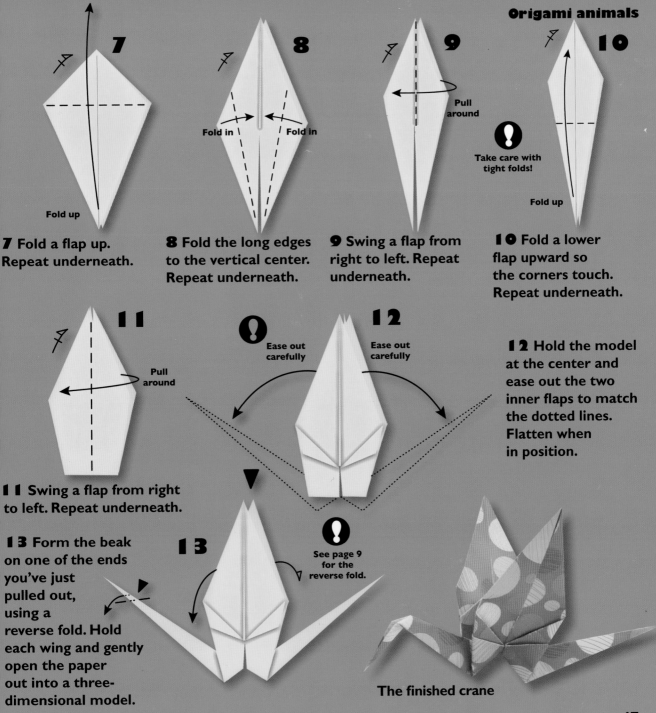

**7** Fold a flap up. Repeat underneath.

**8** Fold the long edges to the vertical center. Repeat underneath.

**9** Swing a flap from right to left. Repeat underneath.

**10** Fold a lower flap upward so the corners touch. Repeat underneath.

**11** Swing a flap from right to left. Repeat underneath.

**12** Hold the model at the center and ease out the two inner flaps to match the dotted lines. Flatten when in position.

**13** Form the beak on one of the ends you've just pulled out, using a reverse fold. Hold each wing and gently open the paper out into a three-dimensional model.

**The finished crane**

47

## How to play Menko

Menko is a Japanese card game played by two or more players. The aim of the game is to win cards from the other players. To win a card, you have to flip it over by throwing your own card at it.

Each player starts with a number of Menko cards made with different colors to avoid confusion. Try with four cards each to start.

Decide who will go first, and all the other players each throw one of their Menko cards onto the ground. The first player throws a Menko card and tries to flip over one of the other cards. If successful, the first player wins the card, and the owner of the flipped card is out of the game.

If the first player fails to flip over any of the Menko cards, the next player gets a turn.

## How to use your fortune teller

To use your model as a fortune teller, start with a square of plain white paper. Color the outside face in four different colors, then number each inside triangle from 1 to 8. Underneath each triangular flap, write a different prediction.

To play, ask a friend to pick a color, then, holding the fortune teller underneath between your fingers and thumbs, open and close it in alternate directions for each letter of the color. Now show your friend inside and ask him or her to pick a number. Again, open and close it in alternate directions to match the number chosen. Finally, choose a number and open the flap to reveal the answer, or your prediction!

## What to do next

Now that you have folded all the models in this book, you will be eager for more models. There is a wealth of material available on the Internet, in both diagram and video form. Why not join a folding society? It's so much fun to fold in a group and others may help you through tricky steps. The two leading societies are:

**Origami USA** www.origamiusa.org
**British Origami Society** www.britishorigami.info

The author's web site is www.origami.me.uk
He also has a facebook page:
www.facebook.com/nicksorigami

## Author's acknowledgments

Fan, bookmark, fish, peacock, frame, four-pointed star created by Nick Robinson. Owl created by Wayne Brown. The other designs are traditional. The author would like to thank the British Origami Society for making me the folder I am today, Wayne Brown for excellent proof-reading, Joan Sallas and the Pooch family for inspiration and friendship, my band Rachel & the Riffs, plus my partner of over 30 years, Ali Robinson and our children Daisy and Nick, not forgetting the cats Matilda and Rhubarb.

# Index

**Picture credits** Key: SS = Shutterstock

Photographs of models on the cover and spreads taken by Nick Robinson. FRONT COVER: Alhovik/SS: (paper for masu box); bekulnis/SS: (papers for crane, purse); EV-DA/SS: (paper for butterfly); martynmarin/SS: (paper for whale); Mrs. Opossum/SS: (papers for envelope, star box); Victoria Kalinina/SS: (paper for fortune teller). BACK COVER: bekulnis/SS: (papers for boat, frame, water bomb); Kaetana/SS: (paper for fish); Kalenik Hanna/SS: (paper for wallet); MeiKIS/SS: (paper for bookmark); Victoria Kalinina/SS: (paper for peacock); Vyazovskaya Julia/SS: (paper for cup); Yulia M./SS: (papers for sailboat, swan). INSIDE COVER – ENVELOPE: Credits listed by papers in columns 1–5, and papers numbered from top to bottom. Column 1, papers 1, 2, 3: Mrs. Opossum/SS; column 2, papers 1, 2, 3: Yulia M./SS; column 2, papers 4, 5, 6, 10, 11: EV-DA/SS; column 2, papers 7, 8, 9: bekulnis/SS; column 3, papers 1, 2: Kaetana/SS; column 3, papers 4, 5, 6: Yulia M./SS; column 3, paper 6: Kalenik Hanna/SS; column 3, paper 7: Alhovik/SS; column 3, paper 8: MeiKIS/SS; column 3, papers 9, 10, 11, 12, 13: WEN WEN/SS; column 3, paper 14: Alhovik/SS; column 3, papers 15, 16, 17: aiym design/SS; column 4, papers 1, 2, 3, 4, 8: bekulnis/SS; column 4, papers 5, 6, 7: Vyazovskaya Julia/SS; column 4, paper 9, 10, 11: Victoria Kalinina/SS; column 5, papers 1, 2, 3: martynmarin/SS. SPREADS: 1: Alhovik/SS: paper for masu box; bekulnis/SS: papers for crane, purse; EV-DA/SS: paper for butterfly; martynmarin/SS: paper for whale; Mrs. Opossum/SS: papers for envelope, star box; Victoria Kalinina/SS: paper for fortune teller. 2: bekulnis/SS: papers for purse, water bomb; martynmarin/SS: paper for whale; Victoria Kalinina/SS: paper for fortune teller; Yulia M./SS: paper for swan. 3: Alhovik/SS: paper for masu box; bekulnis/SS: paper for water bomb; EV-DA/SS: paper for butterfly; Kaetana/SS: paper for fish; Mrs. Opossum/SS: papers for envelope, star box; Victoria Kalinina/SS: paper for fortune teller; Yulia M./SS: paper for sailboat. 5: Nick Robinson; 6: Left, top to bottom: Linda Cole Books Ltd., Yulia M./SS, aiym design/SS, Yulia M./SS, WEN WEN/SS. 6: Right, top to bottom: Alhovik/SS; Mrs. Opossum/SS; bekulnis/SS; bekulnis/SS; bekulnis/SS. 7–47: Nick Robinson: diagrams. 10: aiym design/SS: paper for fan. 11: MeiKIS/SS: paper for bookmark. 13: Vyazovskaya Julia/SS: paper for cup. 14: Kalenik Hanna/SS: paper for wallet. 15: bekulnis/SS: paper for boat. 16–17: Yulia M./SS: paper for sailboat. 18–19: Kaetana/SS: patterned paper for fish. 20–21: martynmarin/SS: paper for whale. 22–23: bekulnis/SS: paper for water bomb. 24: Linda Cole Books Ltd.: paper for Menko model. 25: bekulnis/SS: paper for purse. 26–27: Mrs. Opossum/SS: paper for envelope. 28–29: Alhovik/SS: paper for masu box. 30–31: WEN WEN/SS: paper for box. 32: bekulnis/SS: paper for frame. 34–35: Mrs. Opossum/SS: paper for star box. 36: Linda Cole Books Ltd.: paper for four-pointed star. 38: Linda Cole Books Ltd.: paper for owl. 39: Linda Cole Books Ltd.: paper for puppy. 40–41: EV-DA/SS: paper for butterfly. 42–43: EV-DA/SS: paper for swan. 44–45: Victoria Kalinina/SS: paper for peacock. 46–47: bekulnis/SS: paper for crane.